Frances Turnbull

Published by Musicaliti® Publishers
575 Tonge Moor Road, Bolton, BL2 3BN

Copyright © 2016 Musicaliti
ISBN 978-1-907935-71-8

All rights reserved. No part of this publication may be reproduced, stored in a retrieval system, or transmitted by any means, mechanical, photocopying, recording or otherwise, without the prior permission of the copyright holder.

Index of Songs

Andy Pandy	11
Apple Tree	14
Charlie over the Ocean	26
Chase the Squirrel	15
Come Butter Come	25
G-scale	29
Go Round the Mountain	23
Hey Jim-a-Long	28
Hickory Dickory	9
Hop Old Squirrel	19
Hot Cross Buns	18
I have lost	17
Ickle Ockle	16
Mary had a Little Lamb	20
Old Mister Rabbit	27
On a Log	13
Pease Porridge	10
Poor Little Kitty Cat	24
Riding in a Buggy	21
Rosie Darling	22
Teddy Bear	12

Guitar Basics

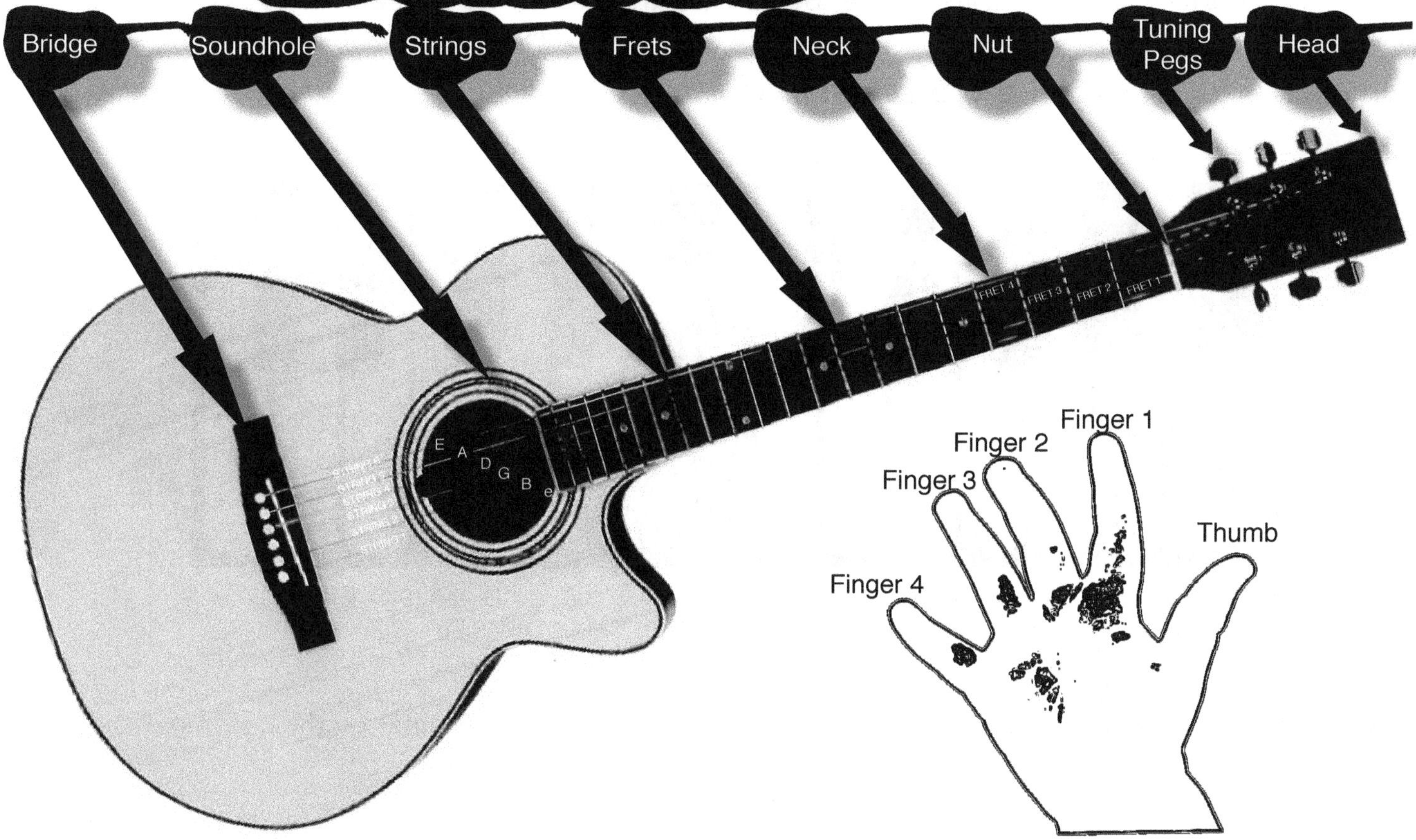

Guitar can be used to play tunes or **melodies** (one or a few notes at a time) or to accompany songs being sung - by playing all the strings with your fingers in the shape of a chord. The songs in this book are all in the chord of G. This means that you can play the G chord and sing along to the songs, or play the tune - it is a great skill to be able to do both! You could even have a guitar friend play the chord while you play the melody (tune) or the other way around! These pictures show the chords that we have used in this book. The numbers in circles show which finger to use!

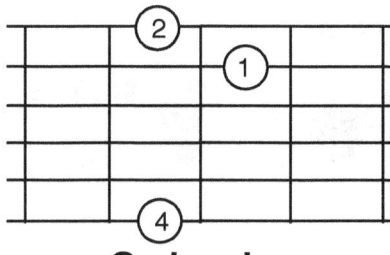
G chord

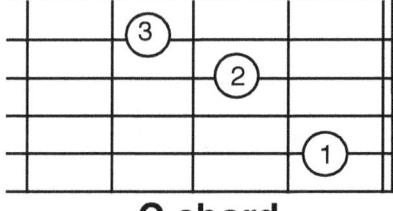
C chord

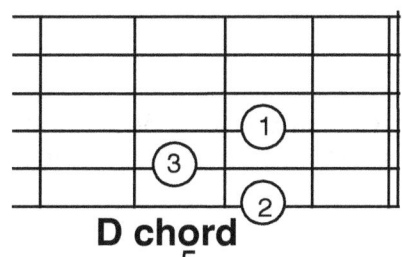
D chord

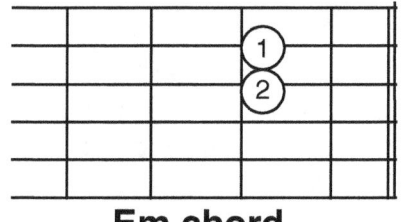
Em chord

How the notes work

The songs in this book are written in the **G scale**. Songs in the **green book** have the fewest notes as you get used to playing the notes of songs on the guitar, with more notes in **pink book**, **yellow book**, **blue book** and **orange book**.

The notes in a G scale are: **G, A, B, C, D, E, F#**. On a **piano**, they look like this:

Music notes: A A# B C C# D D# E F F# G G# A A# B C C# D D# E F F# G G# A
              Bb   Db   Eb   Gb   Ab   Bb   Db   Eb   Gb   Ab

On a **guitar**, they look like this:
(guitar strings start with different notes/letters, and this picture shows the notes on the E string)

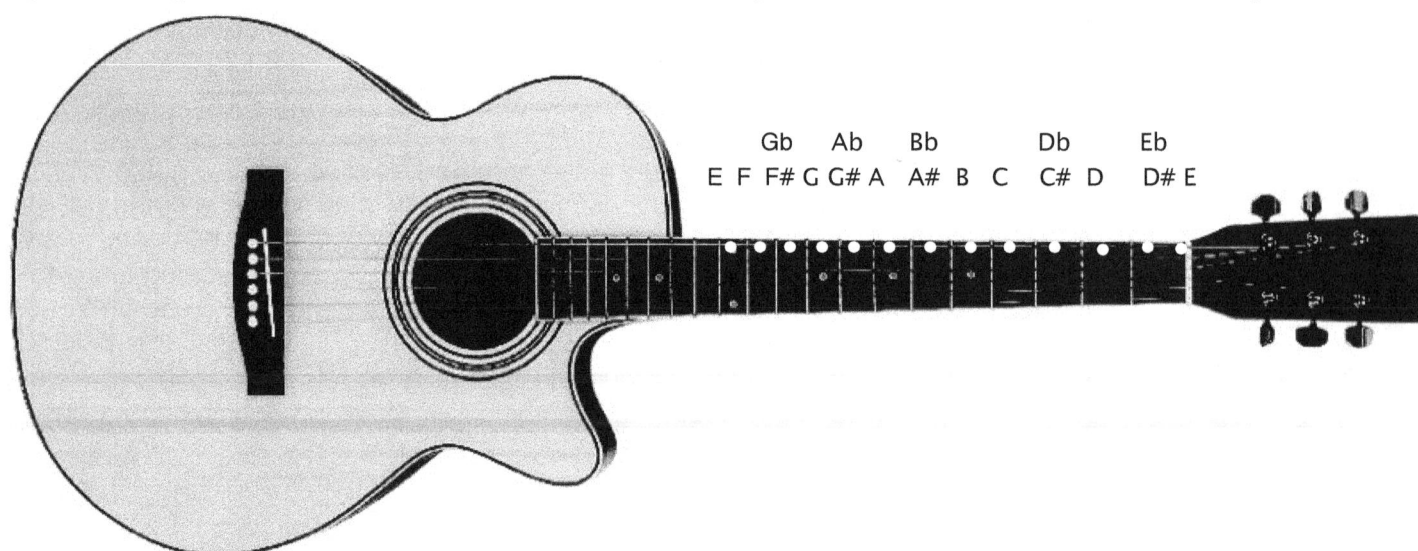

Scales have set gaps in between the notes, and the gaps between these notes determine when the black notes, or sharps and flats (also called accidentals) are used. Accidentals can be sharp (#) or flat (b), depending on the scale.

How the beats work

It's easy to focus on only playing the right notes, but we need to get the **long and short** beats right, too. It can be tricky to work out until we know what the lines and holes in the notes mean, so we can use **movement words** to remember how the beats sound. That way, you could say the movement words instead of the song words to remember how long to play the note!

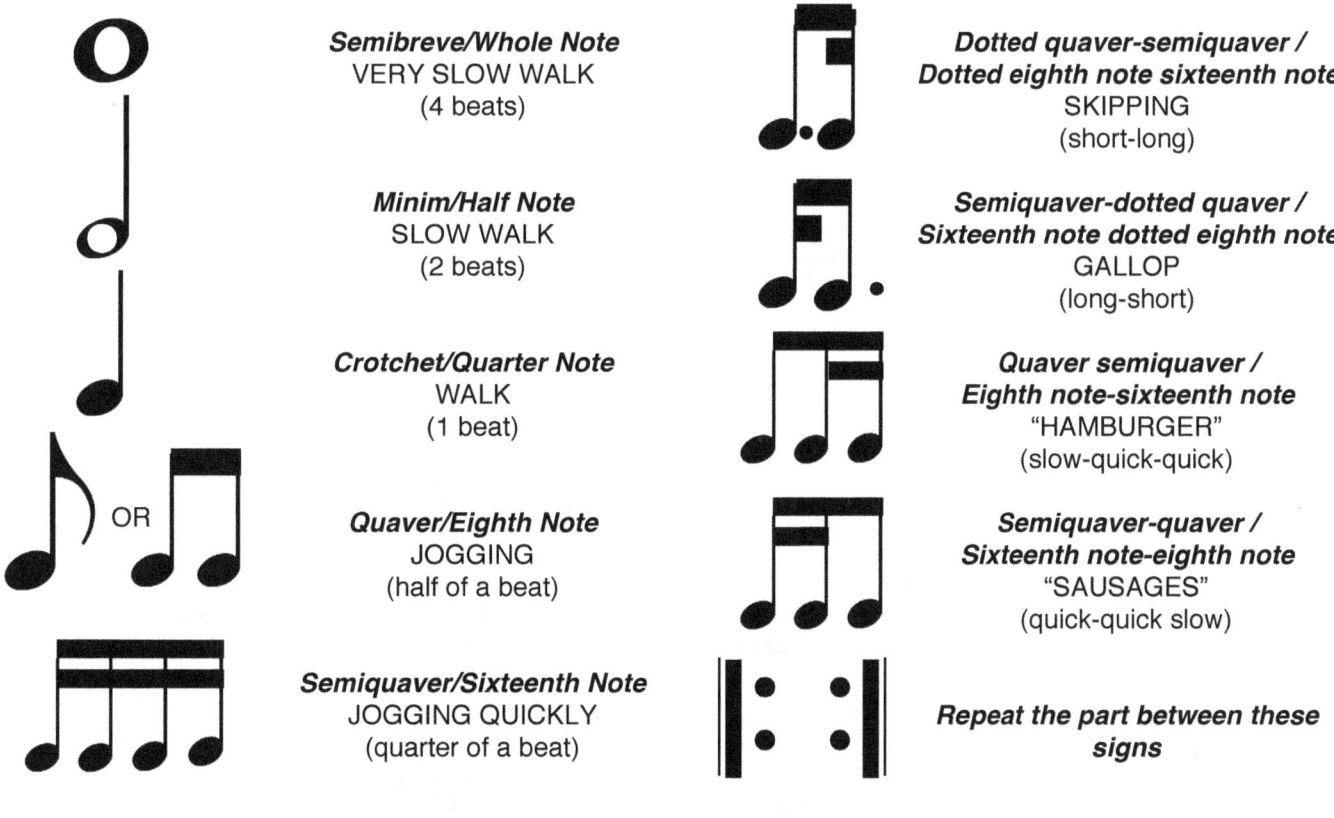

- **Semibreve/Whole Note** — VERY SLOW WALK (4 beats)
- **Minim/Half Note** — SLOW WALK (2 beats)
- **Crotchet/Quarter Note** — WALK (1 beat)
- **Quaver/Eighth Note** — JOGGING (half of a beat)
- **Semiquaver/Sixteenth Note** — JOGGING QUICKLY (quarter of a beat)
- **Dotted quaver-semiquaver / Dotted eighth note sixteenth note** — SKIPPING (short-long)
- **Semiquaver-dotted quaver / Sixteenth note dotted eighth note** — GALLOP (long-short)
- **Quaver semiquaver / Eighth note-sixteenth note** — "HAMBURGER" (slow-quick-quick)
- **Semiquaver-quaver / Sixteenth note-eighth note** — "SAUSAGES" (quick-quick slow)
- **Repeat the part between these signs**

For example, if we sang the movement rhythms to "This Old Man", we would have:

Give it a try before singing the songs!

7

These pages introduce songs with 3 and 4 notes, and the different lengths of beats used:

D is on the 2nd string, 3rd fret
C is on the 2nd string, 1st fret
B is on the 2nd open string
A is on the 3rd string, 2nd fret
G is on the 3rd open string
F# is on the 4th string, 4th fret
D is on the 4th open string

1st string
2nd string
3rd string
4th string
5th string
6th string

Semibreve/Whole Note
VERY SLOW WALK
(4 beats)

Minim/Half Note
SLOW WALK
(2 beats)

Crotchet/Quarter Note
WALK
(1 beat)

Quaver/Eighth Note
JOGGING
(half of a beat)

Semiquaver/Sixteenth Note
JOGGING QUICKLY
(quarter of a beat)

*Dotted quaver-semiquaver /
Dotted eighth note sixteenth note*
SKIPPING
(short-long)

*Semiquaver-dotted quaver /
Sixteenth note dotted eighth note*
GALLOP
(long-short)

*Quaver semiquaver /
Eighth note-sixteenth note*
"HAMBURGER"
(slow-quick-quick)

*Semiquaver-quaver /
Sixteenth note-eighth note*
"SAUSAGES"
(quick-quick slow)

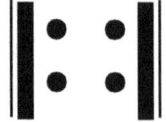

Repeat the part between these signs

8

Guitar Standard Tuning
E-A-D-G-B-E
♩ = 120

Traditional

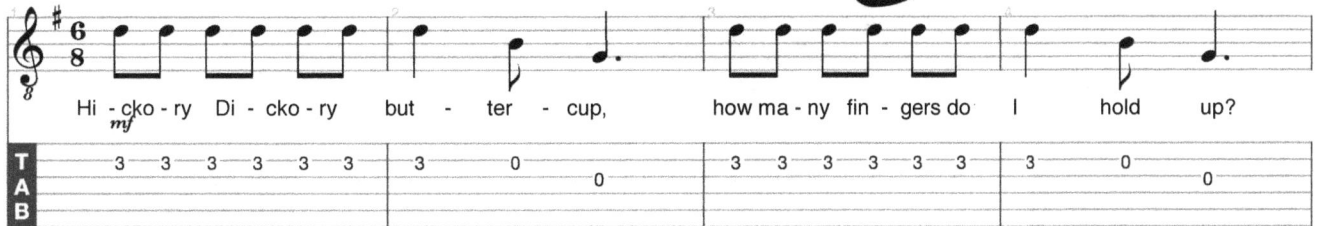

Hi - cko - ry Di - cko - ry but - ter - cup, how ma - ny fin - gers do I hold up?

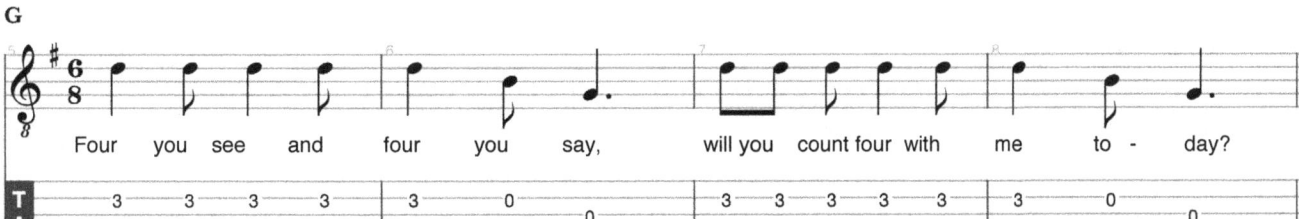

Four you see and four you say, will you count four with me to - day?

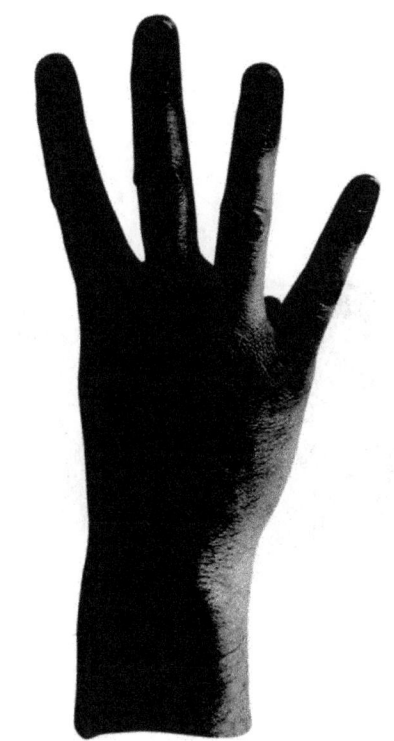

9

Guitar Standard Tuning
E-A-D-G-B-E

♩= 120

Traditional

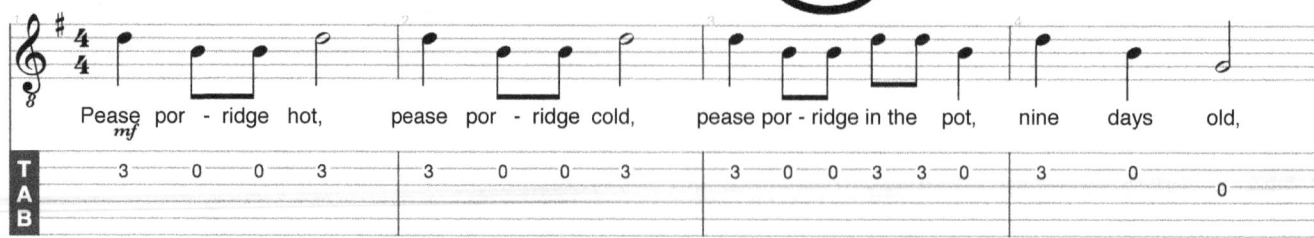

Pease por-ridge hot, pease por-ridge cold, pease por-ridge in the pot, nine days old,

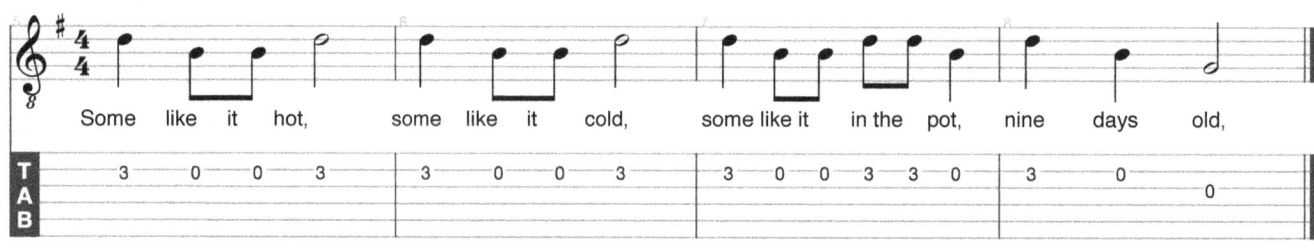

Some like it hot, some like it cold, some like it in the pot, nine days old,

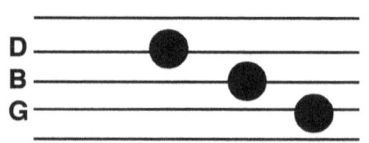

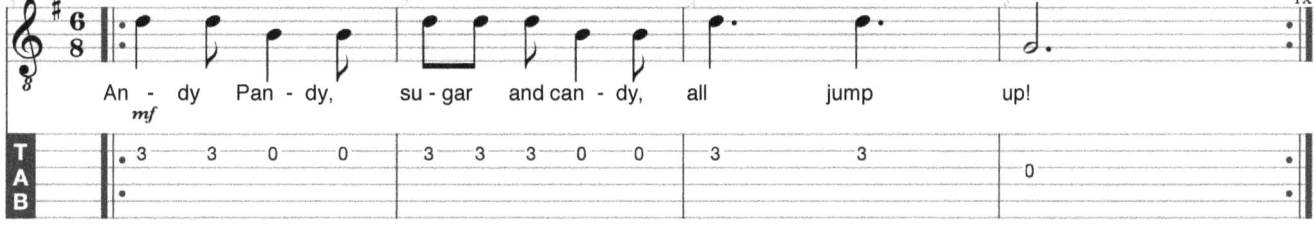

Guitar Standard Tuning
E-A-D-G-B-E
♩ = 120

Traditional

G

An - dy Pan - dy, su - gar and can - dy, all jump up!

Next verse:

Andy Pandy, sugar and candy
All jump down
Andy Pandy, sugar and candy
All jump in
Andy Pandy, sugar and candy
All jump out!

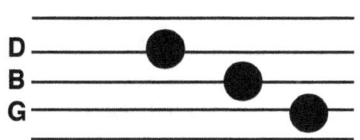

Guitar Standard Tuning
E-A-D-G-B-E

♩ = 120

Traditional

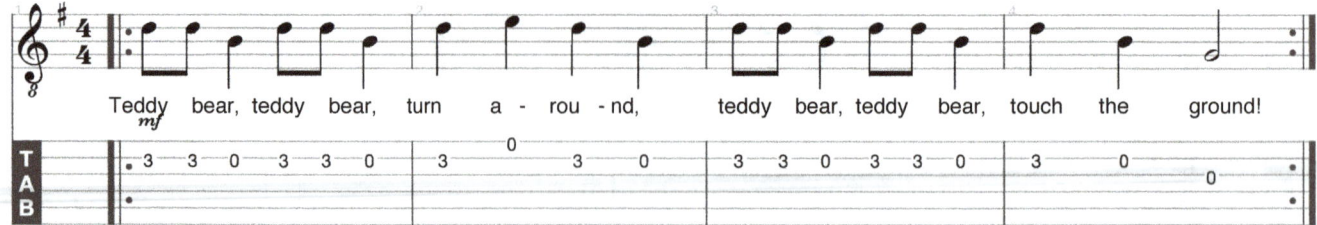

Teddy bear, teddy bear, turn a-round, teddy bear, teddy bear, touch the ground!

Next verses:

Teddy bear, teddy bear
Tie your shoe
Teddy bear, teddy bear
I love you

Teddy bear, teddy bear
Climb the stairs
Teddy bear, teddy bear
Say your prayers
Teddy bear, teddy bear
Turn off the light
Teddy bear, teddy bear
Say goodnight!

12

Guitar Standard Tuning
E-A-D-G-B-E
♩ = 120

Traditional

G

On a log, mis-ter frog, sang his song the whole day long,

Glumpf, glumpf, glumpf, glumpf!

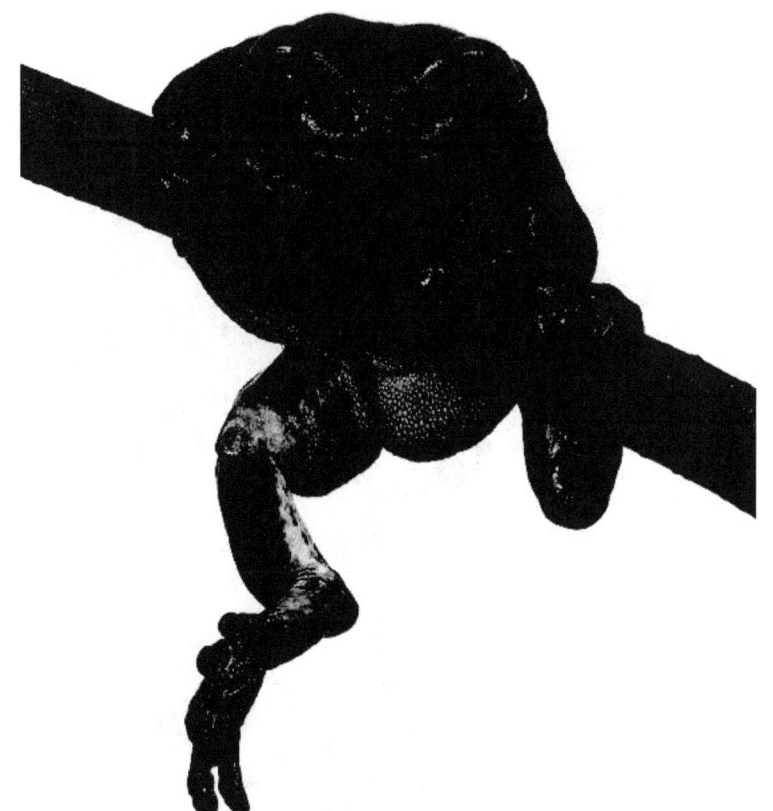

  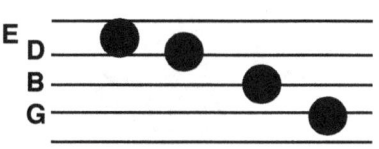

13

Apple Tree

Guitar Standard Tuning
E-A-D-G-B-E
♩ = 120

Traditional

G

Ap - ple tree, ap - ple tree, will your ap - ple fall on me,
mf

```
3   3   0   | 3   3   0   | 3   3   0   0 | 3   3   0
```

I won't cry and I won't shout, if your ap - ple knocks me out!

```
3   3   0   0 | 3   3   0   | 3   3   0   0 | 3   3   0
```

Watch Out!

14

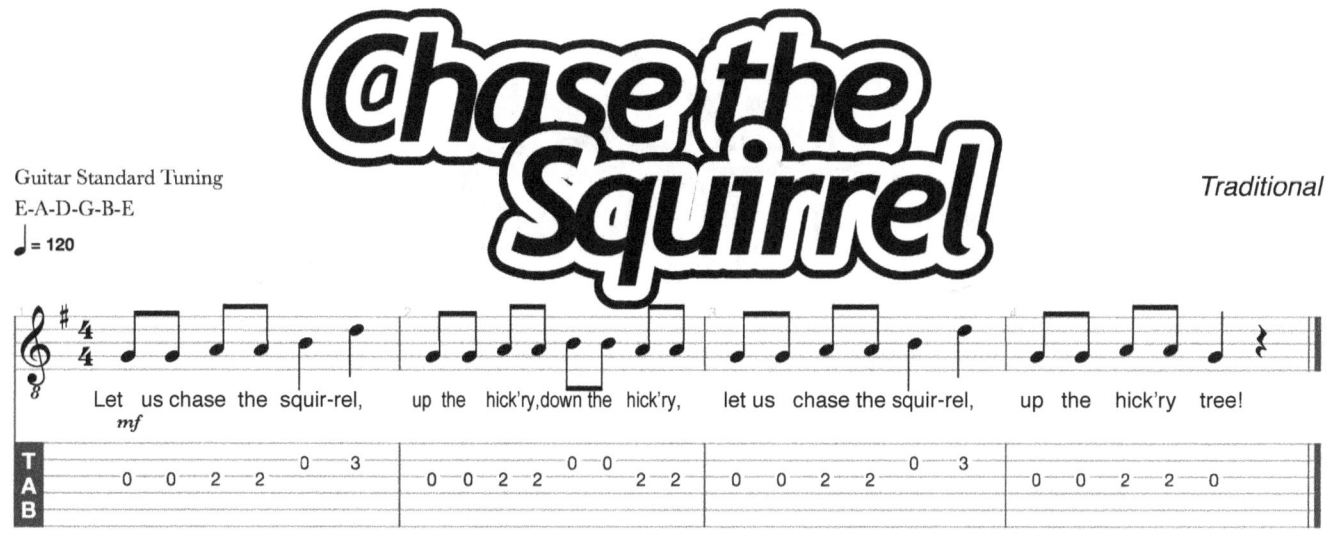

Guitar Standard Tuning
E-A-D-G-B-E
♩ = 120

Traditional

Let us chase the squir-rel, up the hick'ry, down the hick'ry, let us chase the squir-rel, up the hick'ry tree!

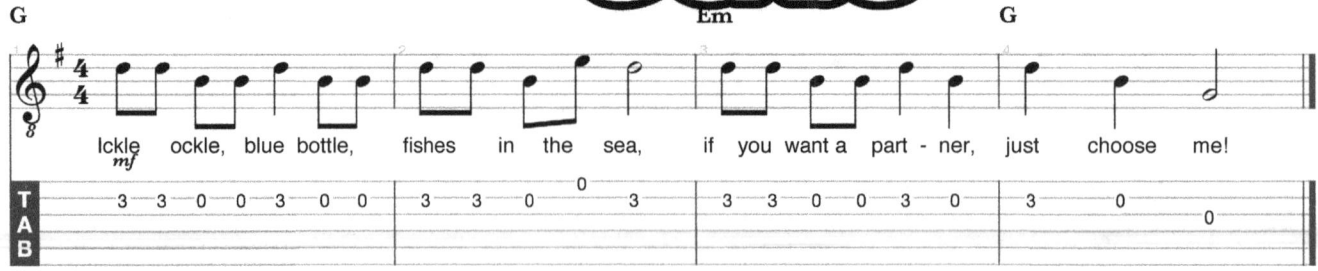

Guitar Standard Tuning
E-A-D-G-B-E
♩ = 120

Traditional

| G | | Em | | G | |

Ickle ockle, blue bottle, fishes in the sea, if you want a part-ner, just choose me!

```
3  3  0  0  3  0  0    3  3  0  3        0  3    3  3  0  0  3  0  3    3    0                0
```

Watch Out! ♩ ♩ ♪♪

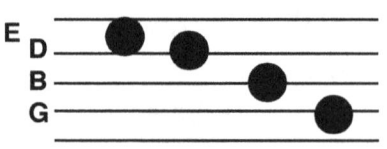

I have lost

Guitar Standard Tuning
E-A-D-G-B-E

♩ = 120

Traditional

I have lost the clo-set key in some la-dies gar-den,

Help me find my clo-set key, in some la-dies gar-den!

  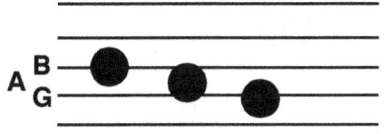

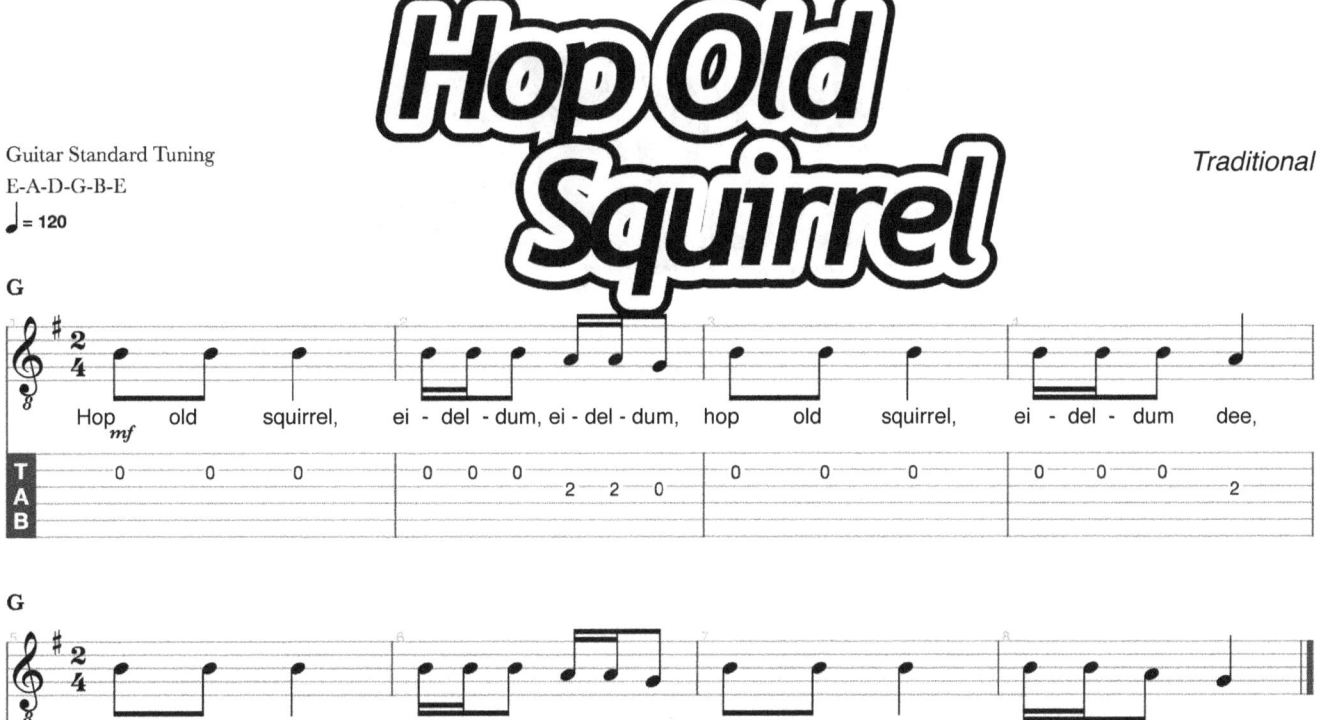

Hop Old Squirrel

Traditional

Guitar Standard Tuning
E-A-D-G-B-E
♩ = 120

Mary had a Little Lamb

Guitar Standard Tuning
E-A-D-G-B-E
♩ = 120

Traditional

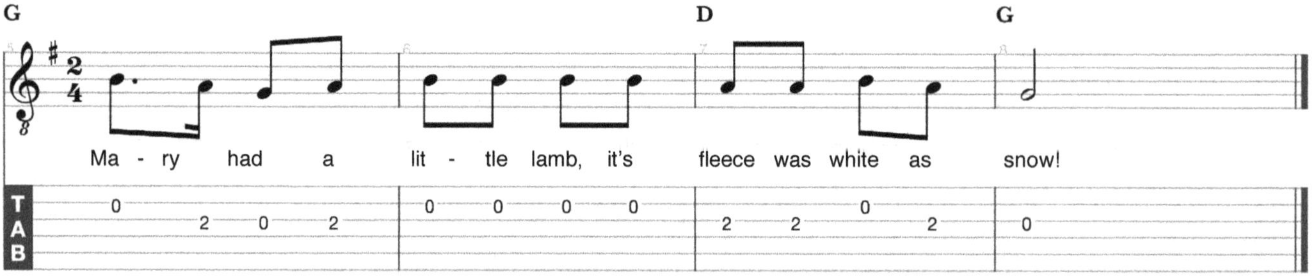

Mary had a little lamb, little lamb, little lamb,
Mary had a little lamb, it's fleece was white as snow!

Next verses:

He followed her to school one day
School one day, school one day
He followed her to school one day
Which was against the rules

It made the children laugh and play
Laugh and play, laugh and play
It made the children laugh and play
To see a lamb at school

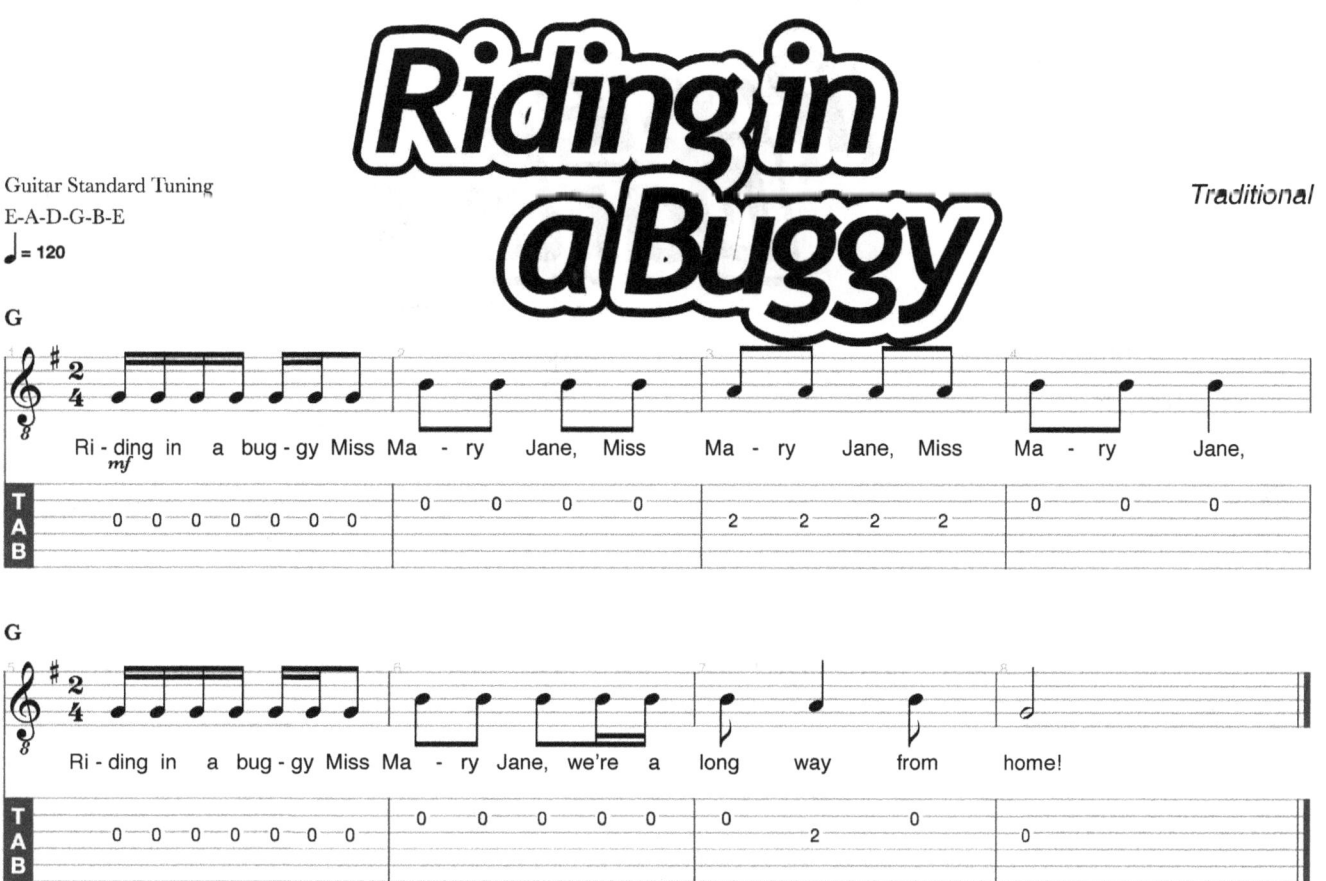

Guitar Standard Tuning
E-A-D-G-B-E
♩ = 120

Traditional

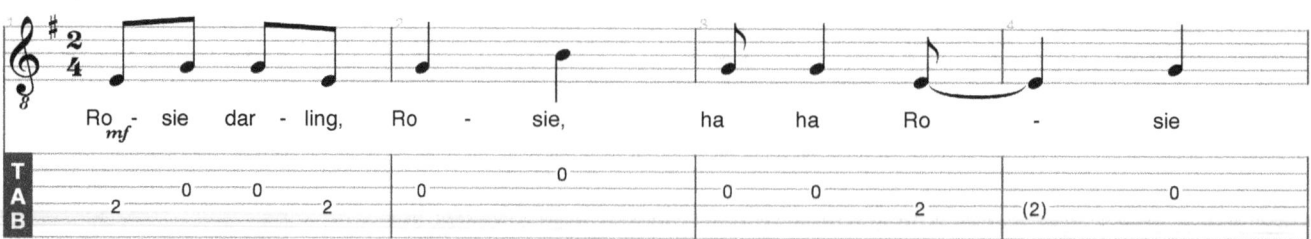

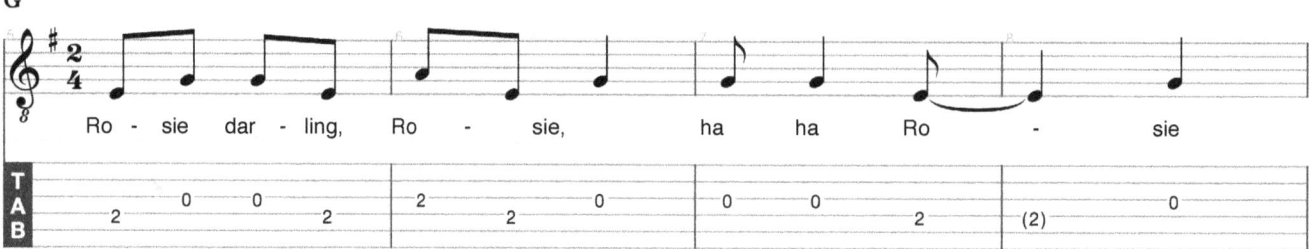

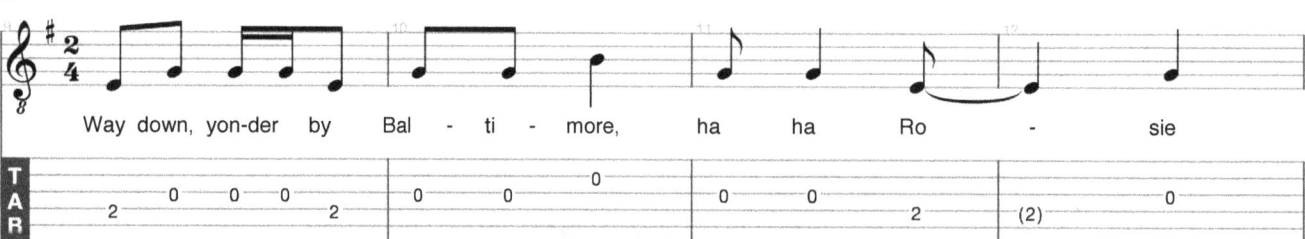

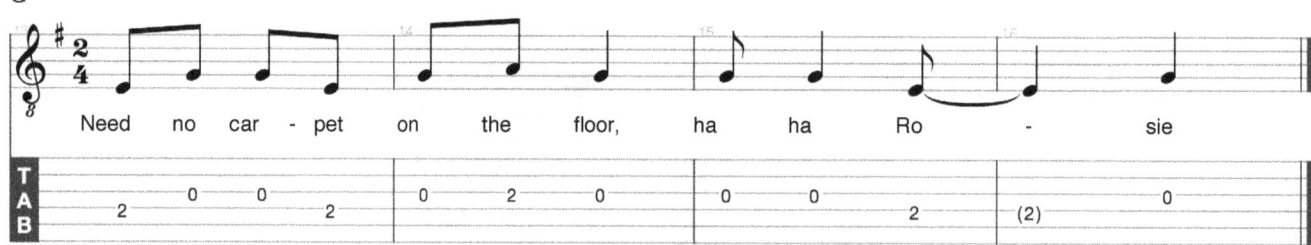

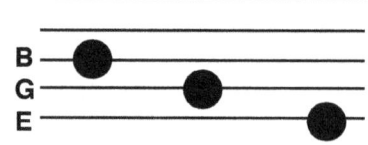

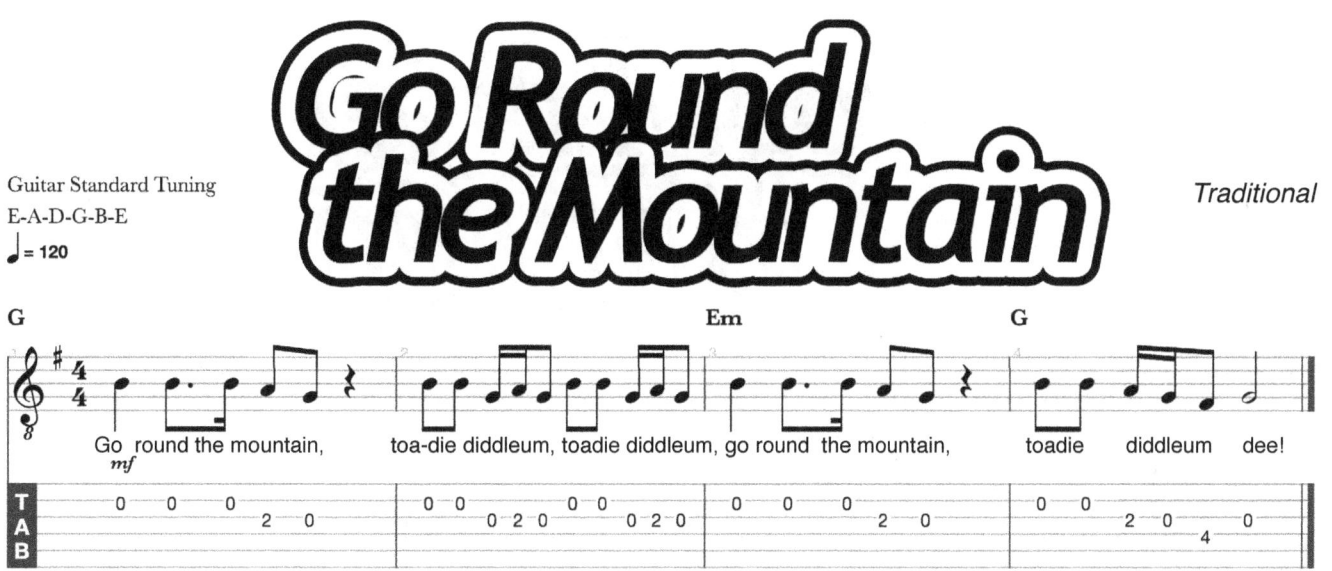

Go Round the Mountain

Guitar Standard Tuning
E-A-D-G-B-E
♩ = 120

Traditional

G — **Em** — **G**

Go round the mountain, toa-die diddleum, toadie diddleum, go round the mountain, toadie diddleum dee!

mf

Next verses:

Tiptoe round the mountain
Toadie, diddle-um, toadie, diddle-um
Tiptoe round the mountain
Toadie, diddle-um, dee

Stomp round the mountain
Toadie, diddle-um, toadie, diddle-um
Stomp round the mountain
Toadie, diddle-um, dee

Skip round the mountain
Toadie, diddle-um, toadie, diddle-um
Skip round the mountain
Toadie, diddle-um, dee

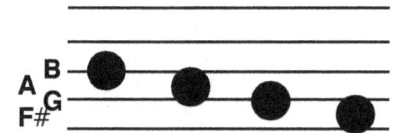

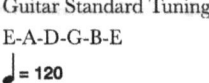

Guitar Standard Tuning
E-A-D-G-B-E
♩ = 120

Traditional

Poor lit - tle kit - ty cat, poor lit - tle fel - ler,

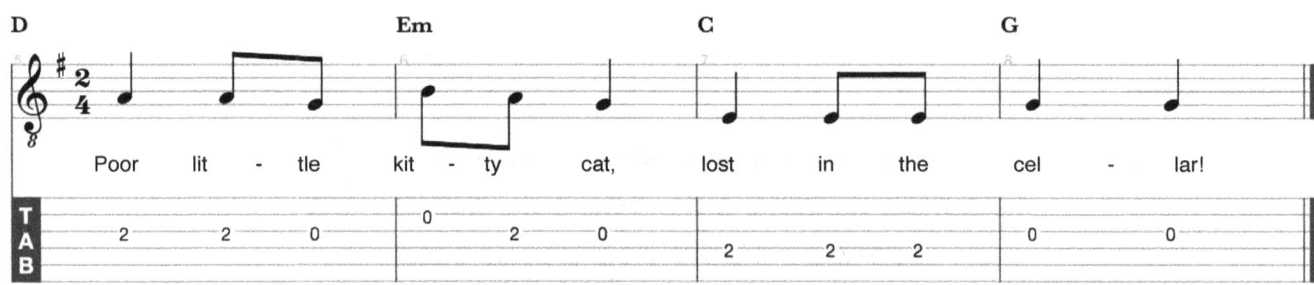

Poor lit - tle kit - ty cat, lost in the cel - lar!

  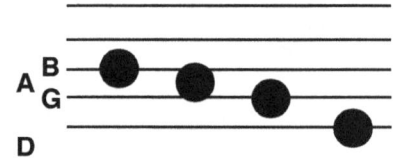

24

Guitar Standard Tuning
E-A-D-G-B-E
♩ = 120

Traditional

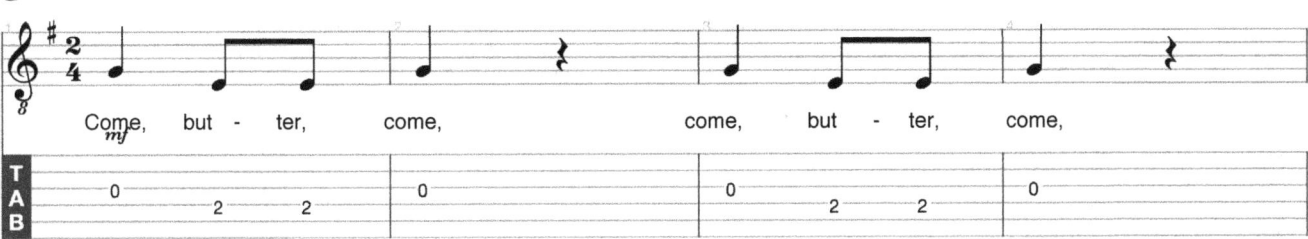

Come, but - ter, come, come, but - ter, come,

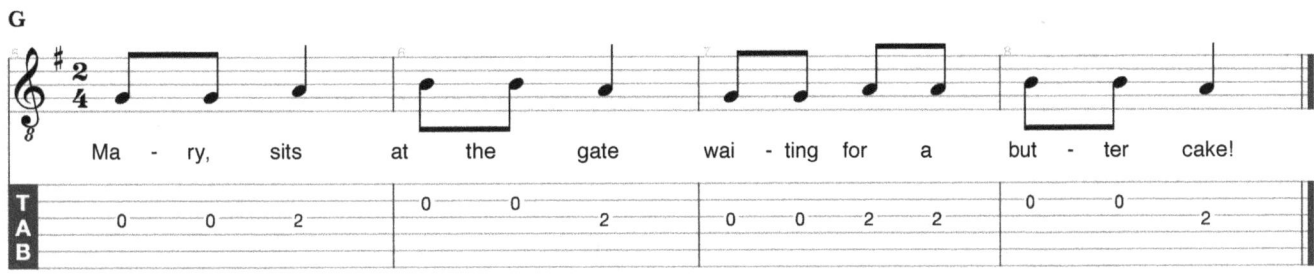

Ma - ry, sits at the gate wai - ting for a but - ter cake!

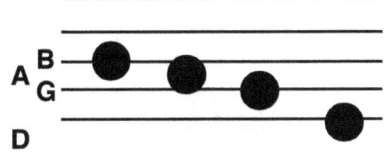

Old Mister Rabbit

Traditional

Guitar Standard Tuning
E-A-D-G-B-E
♩ = 120

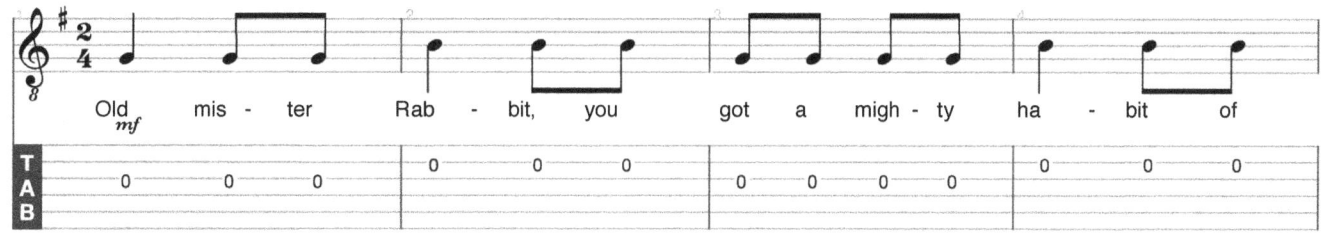

Old mis-ter Rab-bit, you got a migh-ty ha-bit of

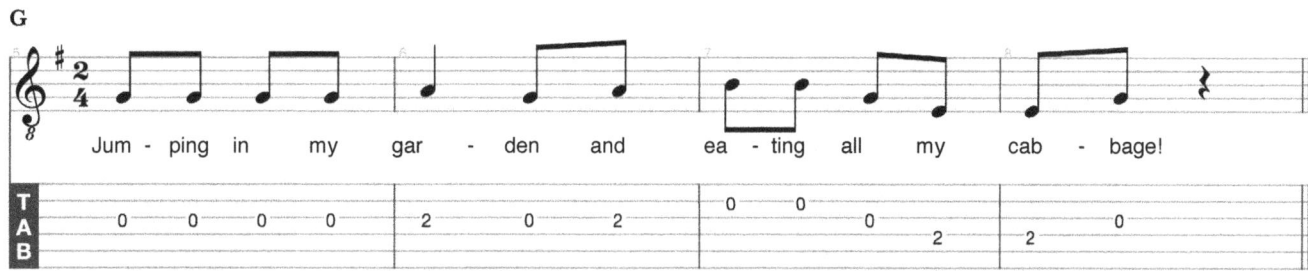

Jum-ping in my gar-den and eat-ing all my cab-bage!

  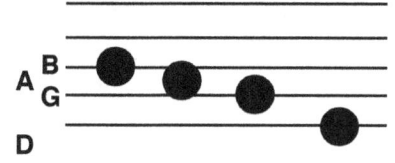

Hey Jim-a-Long

Guitar Standard Tuning
E-A-D-G-B-E
♩ = 120

Traditional

Hey Jim a-long, Jim a-long Jo-sie, Hey Jim a-long, Jim a-long Jo!

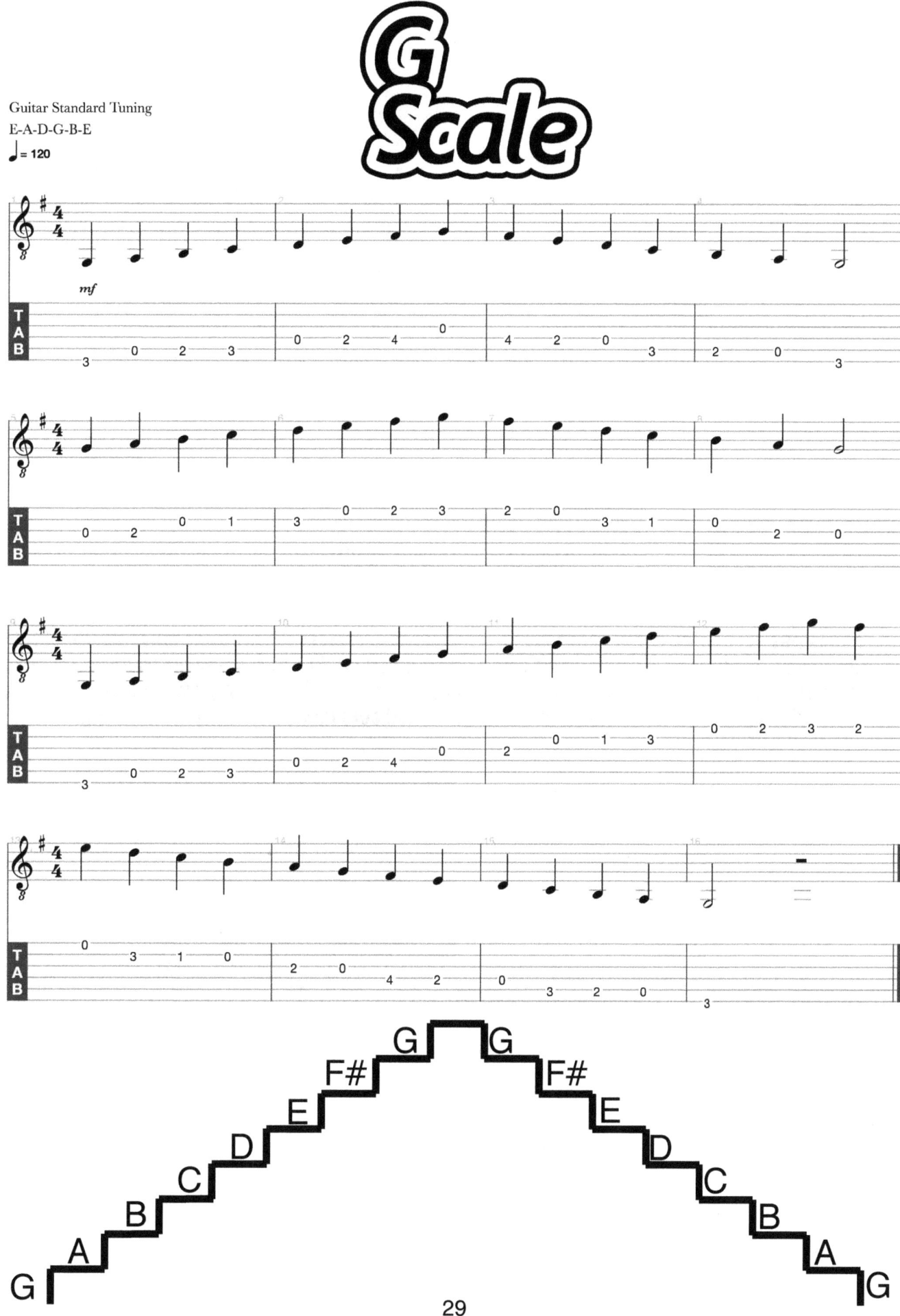

ABOUT THE AUTHOR

Frances has presented early years music sessions in a variety of settings since 2006, after training as a secondary mathematics and science teacher. She is fascinated by research into the health, educational and developmental benefits of music. Not content with being involved with children's music alone, she directs a local community choir, the Warblers.

AVAILABLE TITLES:

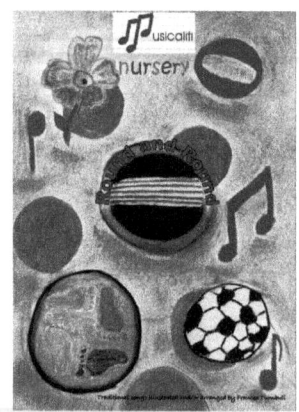

Musicaliti Nursery: Round and Round is a full-colour, illustrated book of well known children's songs for children. Each song includes music rhythms to which children can clap, tap, walk and sing.
ISBN: 978-1-907-935-008

Musicaliti Nursery Series: Magical Musical Kingdom is a full-colour, teaching series of well known and original children's songs with a royal element. Sessions include suggested instruments and activities, with an optional CD of music to purchase or download.
ISBN: 978-1-907-935-152

Musicaliti Nursery Series: Sharks, Fish, Shells is a full-colour, teaching series of well known and original children's songs with a fishy element. Sessions include suggested instruments and activities, with an optional CD of music to purchase or download.
ISBN: 978-1-907-935-169

Musicaliti Nursery Series: Yum, Yum, Yum! is a full-colour, teaching series of well known and original children's songs with a foody element. Sessions include suggested instruments and activities, with an optional CD of music to purchase or download.
ISBN: 978-1-907-935-206

Musicaliti Music Gone Wild is a full-colour, teaching series of well known and original children's songs with an animal element. Using ukulele instruction and chords, play along with your favourite animal songs today!

ISBN: 978-1-907-935-688

Musicaliti Goodies for Guitar is a full-colour, teaching series of well known and original children's songs for beginner guitar. With 90 songs both familiar and unfamiliar, this book covers songs in the scale of G, providing music notation, tablature and guitar chords for accompaniment.
ISBN: 978-1-907-935-206

FORTHCOMING TITLES:

Musicaliti Nursery Series: Balloons, Candles, Cake is a full-colour, teaching series of well known and original children's songs with a party element. Sessions include suggested instruments and activities, with an optional CD of music to purchase or download.
ISBN: 978-1-907-935-190

Musicaliti Nursery Series: Car, bike, plane is a full-colour, teaching series of well known and original children's songs with a transport element. Sessions include suggested instruments and activities, with an optional CD of music to purchase or download.

ISBN: 978-1-907-935-213

Follow Musicaliti **NOW on FaceBook, LInkedIn, ReverbNation, SoundCloud, Twitter and YouTube!**

www.ingramcontent.com/pod-product-compliance
Lightning Source LLC
Chambersburg PA
CBHW081503040426

42446CB00016B/3376